7 SECRETS TO RETIRE RICH

Find Simple and Worry-Free Implementable Ways Inside

7 SECRETS TO RETIRE RICH

Find Simple and Worry-Free Implementable Ways Inside

JIGISH PATEL

Worldwide Published by
Pendown Press

PENDOWN PRESS

An ISO 9001 & ISO 14001 Certi ied Co.,

Regd. O ice: 2525/193, 1st Floor, Onkar Nagar-A,
Tri Nagar, Delhi-110035
Ph.: 09350849407, 09312235086
E-mail: info@pendownpress.com
Branch Office: 1A/2A, 20, Hari Sadan, Ansari Road,
Daryaganj, New Delhi-110002
Ph.: 011-45794768
Website: PendownPress.com

First Edition: 2021

ISBN: 978-93-90828-58-6

Layout and Cover Designed by Pendown Graphics Team
Printed and Bound in India by Th mson Press India Ltd.

CONTENTS

5 FINANCIAL GOALS
YOU SHOULD HAVE

01 EMERGENCY FUND TO FALL BACK ON

02 GET RID OF DEBT COMPLETELY

03 RETIREMENT PLANNING

04 GETTING INSURED

05 CREATE MULTIPLE SOURCES OF INCOME

FOREWORD

Being a retirement strategist, coming from this question must sound strange to you.

In my experience many people just postpone retirement planning.

And there is no specific eason for this delay.

Thus I came up with these solid reasons why you must step on to the journey of Retirement Planning right away:

1. You won't earn forever

Thefirst and obvious reason is that you won't be earning forever. You will eventually retire. The dangerous bit here that people tend to forget is that earnings stop coming but expenses don't.

2. You deserve peace of mind:

You must plan for your retirement phase so you can live with peace and prosperity. Enjoy your hard-earned money. Be able to afford in the future what you actually are working so hard for right now.

Everyone works hard today so that they relax tomorrow. Planning for retirement is the key for ensuring that golden tomorrow.

3. Life is unpredictable

Another major reason to start retirement planning is life is extremely unpredictable. The Pandemic has made this an unforgettable bank.

Unexpected expenses for medical reasons, sudden lay off from jobs, Salary cuts, increase in living costs all these can create a lot stress if you have not invested your money to deal with contingencies.

Retirement planning tends to keep you from falling off the boat in such unforeseen circumstances.

4. Many expenses recur from time to time

To handle major life events that tend to be recurring. Increasing school fees, sudden renovations to your existing home, marriage expenses for kids, repayment of consumer loans, annual vacations, up scaling your vehicles.

All these expenses are always troubling. Th y occur continuously and are unavoidable. So best way to deal with them is to make a financial plan to ensure you can provide for them all with peace of mind.

5. Spend your money and leave some for the kids

Last but definite y not the least, to be able to spend without guilt and leave a legacy for your kids that you love so much.

Many a times I come across clients who have worked very hard all their lives yet they are constantly cutting corners.

Th y haven't planned in time thus they have no savings so they need to live "economically" not by choice but out of sheer lack of funds.

Instead of reaping fruits of their labor, they actually have to deprive themselves.

It's a tendency in India to not spend on yourself but leave behind enough for the children.

No matter how old they actually are. If you want your future self to be able to spend guilt-free and also leave behind a tidy sum for your loved ones then start planning your retirement today. It's that simple.

I am sure my reasons have highlighted that making a retirement strategy is the need of the hour.

Call me or contact me for a free strategy call

I am sure it will be a great way to kick start your financial freedom.

It's just about making the call; rest you can leave it to me.

An expert retirement strategist who can help with the right ideas and plans you may need for a great retired life.

PREFACE

I handhold corporate heads who have less than 10 years left for their retirement to plan for next phase of life in a seamless manner. I have been operating in the Financial Services industry for 20+ years with primary exposure to the Insurance and Investing space. During this journey, I have engaged with 400 + individuals/families.

Reduced working years and enhanced medical advancements have increased the tenure of "retired life stage", thereby making it pertinent to ensure that adequate funds are available to continue to lead a life-after-work without any signifi ant compromise to the desired lifestyle.

Retirement planning requires focus on multiple parameters bifurcated into financial and non-financial My primary focus is on financial parameters, such as risk mitigation, post tax returns & liquidity requirements.

Some of the non-financial parameters could include– succession planning, associated legal aspects, financial records management, personal health management, following passion and few more. That is exactly why about 400+ top corporate leaders in Mumbai trust me with their retirement planning.

I engage with my clients' directly and usually on board only 25 new clients in a year to ensure I give my clients highly personalized & confidential se vice.

–Jigish Patel

Chapter I

THE MANTRA

> *"Nothing ever just happens. You have to make it happen, including individual success. Success is a direct result of definite action, carefully planned and persistently carried out by the person who has conditioned his mind for success and believes he will attain it."*
>
> **-Napoleon Hill**
>
> *(World Renowned Author)*

This in a nutshell is the "mantra" for life. Here are three simple steps to execute from this mantra.

1. Read
2. Understand
3. Apply

Simply put, to be successful in any phase of life, planned and persistent actions are a must.

*"Make Everything As Simple
As Possible, But Not Simpler."*

-Albert Einstein

Chapter II

UNDERSTANDING RETIREMENT

The dictionary meaning of retirement is "the action or fact of leaving one's job and ceasing to work." You could be retiring by choice or by a mandatory cap.

Simply put, it is that phase of life where you will no longer be working either by choice or mandate. It's the longest vacation plan of your life and incidentally, nobody else will finance it under any circumstances. Hence, planning for it is extremely crucial. Especially, if you don't want to depend on anyone else for your own lifestyle choices and expenses.

As per a survey conducted on Retirement Readiness in India, only 36% "think" that they are on course. A majority of working Indians do not believe they are on track to achieving their required retirement income.

That brings us to the ultimate question

How much do you need for retirement?

The e is no one-size-fits-a l formula that comes up with the golden number for an Individual. Don't worry, as you have already embarked upon the journey of reading this guide, which will help you demystify all that you need to know about retirement planning.

According to research nearly 68% of the working age population expects their children to support them in their retirement, usually due to their unpreparedness. In reality, only 30% retirees are actually getting such financial & emotional support.

Chapter III

ASK THE RIGHT QUESTIONS

Have you thought how much money you will need for a comfortable and financia ly independent life post retirement?

The ans ers could be:

A. Yes, I know how much I need. (Awesome – Do you regularly monitor your investments?)

B. No, I have been thinking about it but haven't got time for it yet. (Prioritize today)

C. No, Why? Should I even think about it now, as I am only X years of age? (Think n w)

D. No, I don't have enough savings left every month. (Let's plan)

If you chose B, C, or D, that's great. You must be thinking how that is great when you actually have no planning for retirement. You can start now. It is not that late yet!

Also, this concise guide will help you Retire Rich.

In a most simple and lucid manner, the next few pages will take you through a journey of retirement planning. This simple to understand jargon-free guide will help you towards planning.

We succeed only as we identify in life, or in war, or in anything else, a single overriding objective, and male all considerations bend to that one objective.

What do people think of retirement?

Estimates Age for Retirement? 50-69
Almost 80% of respondents ages 25-44 chose a retirement age in this band. The majority want to retire before 60.

How much is needed? 59% says don't know
Although 65% are already saving for retirement, most didn't have a clue about the cost of retirement living.

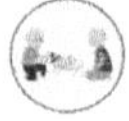

Will you Afford current Lifestyle? 48% say No
There is a growing realization that life gets tough after regular income stops.

Where to invest? 52% say traditional investment Traditional investment options are not enough to beat inflation.

Equity or Debt? 61% don't know
Respondents are not aware about the importance of asset allocation in retirement planning.

Considering a Financial Advisor? 77% say No
This is a worrying fact, considering the limited knowledge on the right investment options or retirement planning.

"Retirement is the Beginning."

Chapter IV

7 MISTAKES OF RETIREMENT PLANNING

What are these 7 common mistakes that many individuals make in pre retirement phase? This guide will help you quickly identify if you are one of them and if so, how to rectify the same.

1. **Underestimating income needs during retirement stage:** A majority of individuals have no or limited clue of the approximate amount they would need to live a financia ly independent life post-retirement. Retirees tend to spend on different things considering their lifestyle.

2. **Health care expense assessment:** In today's fast-paced life, keeping good health is often a tedious task. Medical treatment costs burn not just one but several holes in your pockets. Plan and avail a health insurance plan that will cover potential medical expenses including any hospitalization especially during later stages of

life, especially when income levels will be relatively subdued.

3. **Concentrated investments:** Every investment type, be it financial and/or non- financial equity and/or debt; have their own role to play in the overall returns of a portfolio. Diversifi ation is pivotal for a successful, steady and stable investment basket. As the proverb goes–Do not put all eggs in one basket.

4. **Inconsistency in tracking investments:** 2020 has taught us about unpredictability - anything can happen anytime. Many such factors demand that one keeps a watchful eye on their savings and investment pattern and plan and keep it dynamic.

   Adopt the triple A approach - Analyze-Assess-Adapt. Re-examining the retirement plan at regular intervals will ensure that it stays dynamic, thereby making your retirement goals remain achievable.

5. **Debt troubles:** Long-term debts such as home loans, property loan, vehicle loans, and payment of monthly EMI's for various long- and short-term investment goals linked with children's education or marriage, buying second home, etc., will take a major chunk from your monthly income, at least till they are fully repaid.

6. **Ignoring the impact of inflation:** Inflati n is a demon that comes down hard on anyone who ignores it. Since, retirement is a long-term goal, it is important to understand the impact of inflati n on your financial goals. Inflati n is the rate at which general prices of products and services in the market rise. It reduces purchasing power substantially.

Assuming 7% inflati n, 1,00,000 today will be worth 13,000 after 30 years. Other way round, your monthly expenses of 1,00,000 today will be worth 7,60,000 after 30 years.

7. **Funds access and liquidity planning:** Building wealth will require you to devote substantial sums to your future. This strategy seems obvious, but many individuals seem to be oblivious of it. In order to be able to save and invest for retirement, you should be spending less than you earn - and definite y not trying to keep up with the peers. Tha 's how you generate funds for investing.

Once you have surplus funds, you need a robust investment plan. The earlier you start investing for retirement, the better. Reap the benefits of power of compounding. The example below shows what a difference even fi e years can make.

If at 30 or 40 you're thinking that you can just put off investing for a few years, you might end up with several lakhs of rupees less in retirement because of that delay.

Pro Tip

Ensure you invest in a planned manner so you can access funds when you need them. Liquidity management is very essential when you plan for retirement.

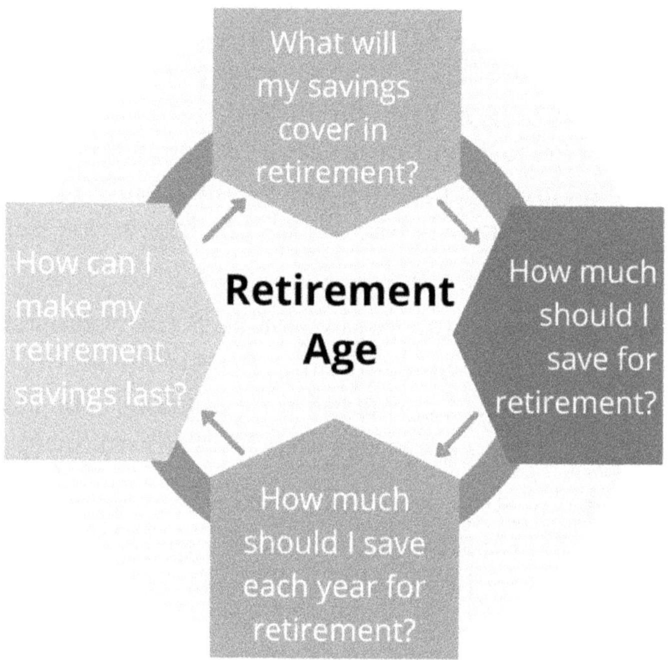

"The Ultimate Security Is Your Understanding Of Reality."

Chapter V

7 LIFE LESSONS TO RICH RETIREMENT

When you read the common mistakes in the earlier chapter, you must have related to a few of them. Once you know what the deterrent is in your retirement planning journey, it's easier to deal with it.

Before we delve into what and how to do now for retirement planning ideas, I want to share a story.

It's a real-life story of a janitor in the USA who made millions. Yes, a simple janitor became a Millionaire. He would have earned wages that were not extremely high. So, what was his secret for making millions?

Ronald Read was born in rural Vermont, a state in the north eastern United States. He was the first person in his family to graduate high school. Read died in 2014, aged 92. Which is when the humble rural janitor made international headlines?

28, 13, 503 Americans died in 2014. Fewer than 4,000 of them had a net worth of over $8 Million when they passed away. Ronald Read was one of them. In his will the former janitor left $2 million to his step-kids and more than $6 million to his local hospital and library.

There was no secret. There was no lottery win. Read saved what little he could and invested it in blue chip stocks. Then for decades on end, as tiny savings compounded into more than $8 million, Read just waited. He stayed invested over a long term.

We must learn 7 life lessons from Read's story.

1. No matter how much you earn you can retire rich
2. A frugal lifestyle will make you rich.
3. Never spend money recklessly. Value your earnings.
4. Choose to save and invest your savings.
5. Build a diversified portfolio of stocks with concentration in quality assets.
6. Compounding works.
7. You have to let it work.

There is no Get Rich Quick option.

"Never raid your retirement nest egg, even when adversity strikes, you get laid off, run into health problems, fund college, or get divorced."

Chapter VI

7 STEPS TO RICH RETIREMENT

1. **Track your net worth and spending:** Continue to track your net worth to ensure being stuck on the path of financial independenc .
2. **Cut down on unwanted expenses:** Be clear of your needs & wants.
3. **Save your raises:** Save and invest your money before spending it.
4. **Take regular inventory of your finances:** Calculate your Net-worth & your annual expenses.
5. **Create alternative income sources:** Th ough side-hustles or investments, enhancing your skill set, finding a passi n that pays.
6. **Raise money-savvy children:** If your children grow up relatively clueless about money management, they can end up needing a lot more financial support throughout their adult lives, thus affecting your retirement corpus.

7. **Get and stay healthy:** This may seem a weird advice for retiring rich. If you're not very healthy as you approach and enter retirement, you may spend a lot of money on doctor visits, test, treatments, medications, and possibly more. It's no secret that healthcare is expensive and costs are ever increasing. Even medical advancements are happening, whereby human life is getting elongated.

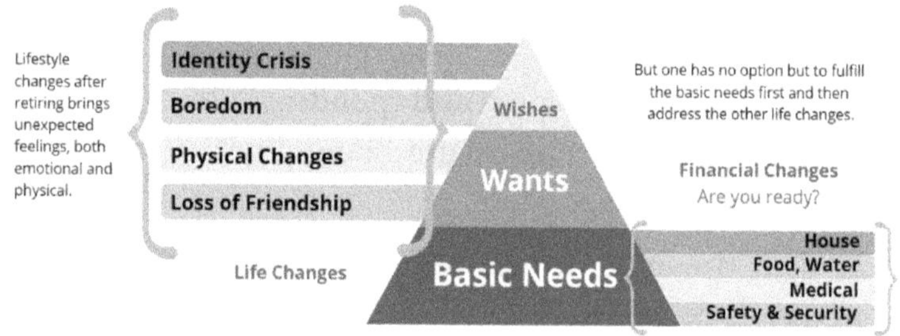

Pro Tip

Taking care of your health is the best way of Taking care of your Wealth.

"If you ask what is the single most important key to longetivity, I would have to say it is avoiding worry, stress, and tension. And if you didn't ask me, I's still have to say it."

Chapter VII

7 SECRETS FOR A RICH RETIREMENT

Secret #1 – Courage and Conviction

Courage to be patient during the upheavals of the stock markets and macro-economic conditions. We already have seen the havoc the pandemic has created and the light at the end of the tunnel is still dim. Having said, the stock markets have bounced back with a bang.

The fall and rise of the stock markets exemplified that if you are invested in the right assets (e.g., equities) all you have to do is maintain courage and conviction.

Retirement corpus is built over a long-term period. Only then you will be able reap rich rewards. TheRonald Read story provides ample evidence of it. Staying put and patient will yield rich rewards.

Secret #2 – Asset Allocation

This is the co nerstone of a successful retirement plan.

Getting the right mix is the magic ingredient. A diversified portfolio, ideally, will yield returns consistently, provide capital security and timely liquidity. If this is done correctly financial freedom will not remain a dream, it will be your Retirement reality.

The i lustration provides a clearer picture.

ASSET ALLOCATION

Growth & Capital Appreciation	Regular Income	Liquidity	Capital Preservation
• Equity Share • Equity Mutual Funds • Gold ETF • Real Estate	• FDs • Bonds • Debt Funds • Real Estate	• Short term FDs • Liquid, Overnight, Low Duration & Short Duration • Debt Mutual Funds	• Short term FDs • Liquid & Debt Funds • Post Office/NSC • PPF

ASSET ALLOCATION OPTIONS

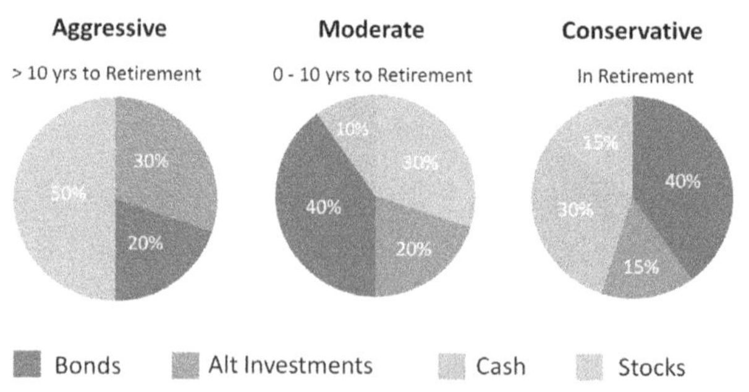

Secret #3 – Diversification

How many of you feel your home is an asset? It's definite y a good investment and gives you a sense of security. Investment in property is considered prudent but only if you get it at the right price and time.

Property investments are non liquid. Especially in times of crisis you cannot liquidate unless you opt for a distress sale. The return on capital is also poor as rentals yield incomes lower than fi ed deposits especially in cities like Mumbai. (See illustration to understand better)

Diversifi ation is crucial. Monitoring the asset allocation dynamically and ensuring ongoing diversifi ation will ensure the required rate of return is maintained. This then leads to a high growing portfolio.

Thishelps to ensure that the retirement corpus is achieved.

The key is to find the right balance. It's an art that needs practice and experience.

This is where consulting a niche Retirement Planner can prove to be a prudent decision as such a planner can provide you a hawk eye view of every aspect of building a retirement corpus.

Secrets #4 – Cultivate consistent saving and investment habits

Age old wisdom, gold standard advice, simple, uncomplicated. Need of the hour. We are at the peak of consumerism. Everyone is trying to sell you products you don't need every moment of the day via social media. Worst is the next generation is addicted. In a matter of few clicks, instant gratifi ation at the cost of peace of mind. This has also resulted in a surge in unproductive debts for so many families.

Saving for a rainy day has never been so relevant, the current pandemic proved it. Not having access to contingency fund has proved to be a challenge for many families.

Only saving can help you a little. It's planned investing of savings that leads to wealth creation. Develop this habit in yourself and your children, as early as you can, as little as you can. In the long run this will make a difference. Getting rich starts with self discipline and self control. Are you ready for it?

Secret #5 – Creation of a sound inheritance plan

Everyone loves their family. If anyone has experienced family disputes, they understand the stress it creates, financial as well as emotional, especially the uncomfortable conversations around it. Spare your family the pain. Create your will and ideally get it registered. Remember a probate, to execute the will, is required in a few geographies in India, including Mumbai.

A sturdy inheritance plan will ensure your loved ones remain happy and conflict f ee even after you are gone.

Retirement planning will ensure you plan not only your future, but even that of your family. Leave a mark of your sincere care for your loved ones by preparing a WILL.

Secret #6 – Consider the Impact of Inflation

When you plan your retirement corpus this is one factor that is of utmost importance. Inflati n impacts your future purchasing power.

Inflati n is like an acorn. It starts out small, but given enough time, can turn into a mighty oak tree. We've all heard—and want—compounded growth of our money. Well, inflati n is like 'compound anti-growth,' as it erodes the value of your money.

A seemingly small inflati n rate of 5% will erode the value of your savings by more than 50% over approximately 30 years. Doesn't seem like much each year, but given enough time, it has a huge impact. See the illustrations to gain a better understanding of inflati n.

Secret #7 – The Magic of compounding

Compounding is the culmination of time and arithmetic. The treasure this combination can spin over a long term is a reality. This again was also present in the real-life story of Ronald Read.

Example: 1

Rs. 10,00,000 invested for 20 yrs @ ROE of 12% is Rs.96,46,293

Rs.10,00,000 invested for 40 yrs @ ROE of 12% is Rs.9,30,50,970

The power of compounding though considered to be a common knowledge yet seldom harnessed. See the illustrations for better understanding.

Remember: Compounding only works if you can give an asset time to grow.

It's like planting oak trees (a thought - you may wish to give example of mango tree, as not sure how many of your readers would have seen an oak tree). A year of growth will never show much progress, 10 years can make a meaningful difference, and 50 years can create something absolutely extraordinary.

Remember: Getting and keeping that extraordinary growth requires surviving all the unpredictable ups and downs that everyone inevitably experiences over time. Theyear 2020 is an example where if you had panicked on account of the stock market fall post pandemic announcement, your long terms return would have been impacted severely. Today the stock markets have bounced back and how?

Compounding is not just about high return on investments. It is steady returns sustained uninterrupted for the longest period of time - especially in times of chaos and havoc - you will always win.

Statistics don't work when you're a sample size of one.

No amount of planning or statistical analysis can overcome future unknowns. The best solution is to build your budget based on your unique plan for retirement.

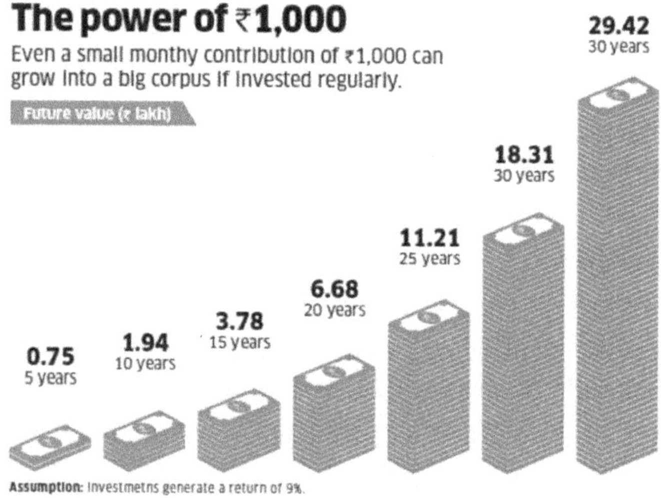

Early start pays off over time

Investing more in the initial years can reduce burden on income in future.

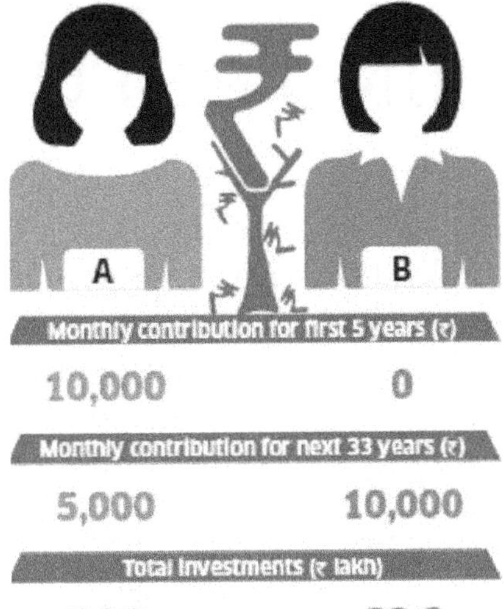

Final corpus at 60 years (₹ crore)

2.51 2.44

Assumptions: Started working at 22 and got married at 27; investmetns generated a return of 9%

Bonus Chapter

RETIREMENT PLANNING CHECKLIST

Most individuals have various ideas regarding retirement. The e is, however, a common concern: most people want the choice of when to stop working. The e is a big difference in working because you want to work and working because you have to work.

If you want a choice then you must think about it now. The e is no better moment than today. Optimize the power of now!

Regarding your retirement income needs, do you wish to

1. Live off inc me, preserve capital? or
2. Live off income & capital, no need to preserve assets for any inheritance or
3. Live off income & capital, but want to leave some assets as part of inheritance

4. Do fi l out the checklist to get a fair idea of where you currently stand.

The Ultimate Questions to ask yourself to plan for having fulfi ling retirement.

1. Have you thought of retirement?
2. At what age would you like to retire?
3. How the retirement life should be?
4. Do you want to pursue any unrealized personal goal or any personal hobby?
5. Would this require any capital outfl w?
6. Is it important for you to have all debt, liability, paid off p ior to retirement?
7. What is it going to take, to make sure you can retire when you want to?
8. What are you presently doing to ensure you can retire as per your plan?
9. What is the existing corpus already made?
10. Are you satisfied about the quality of assets year marked for your retirement?
11. Balance Required
12. Time Lag in years
13. How much you invest for retirement?

7 Step Plan For Retirement

- Determine Your Retirement Needs
- Estimate Your Retirement Income
- Calculate Your Expenses
- Develop A Savings Plan
- Follow Asset Allocation
- Network Through Social Media
- Evaluate Your Health

"Your Retirement Number Is Only As Accurate As The Assumptions Behind It."

FROM
THE EXPERT'S DESK

Jigish Patel is a Retirement strategist with years of exposure in this field cross multiple individuals & families.

A man with a solid vision of ensuring your Retirement is as prosperous and fulfi ling as it can be.

Dedicated extensive research to give prudent and customized retirement plans.

The info graphic depicts his simple yet sensible ideas for leading a happy and fulfi ling retirement life.

Find your IKIGAI (Japanese for "value of being alive") with him.

TESTIMONIALS

Whether you are in trouble or you want to hasten the process of growing your wealth for a secure and comfortable post- retirement life, Jigish Patel is the best financial advisor in his niche. Very objective, very informed, and very sharp. A short look at your portfolio and he is able to tell you what improvements you can make for better growth.

A good thing about him is that he doesn't promise you the stars. Thisis what I liked when I talked to him for the first time. I was having trouble growing my finances as in my mid years, I ignored retirement planning. You can easily say that when I talked to him for the first time, I had zero investments for retirement. I was suddenly in a panic mode.

He comforted me by saying that no matter how bad the situation seems, there is always a way out. He analyzed my investments, however much they were, and suggested changes with real-time calculations. I could literally see in front of my eyes where I was losing money and where I could make more money. I was immediately sold.

Rahul Ghosh,

Rahul Ghosh, Motor Spare Parts Supplier

When I had started investing money for my retirement in early 2000's I thought I was taking sufficien steps to make my old age secure and comfortable. Then other pressing matters of everyday life took precedence and for almost a decade I ignored my investments. Some of them stagnated, some showed a bit of growth, and some were in the red. It wasn't like I was careless, it's just that, in the absence of a being a qualified investor, I lost track.

Fortunately, somewhere around 2014 I met Jigish. Even during the first meeting, he completely changed my perception towards how to invest and how not to invest. He has an uncanny ability to just throw a glance at your investments and know how much you have saved and how much you are going to save in the coming years.

I have gained the lost ground with his help. This wouldn't have been possible on my own. I'm looking towards a happier and contented old-age, and in fact, I strongly believe that I will have a great time, thanks to him.

Ganesh Majumdar,
Regional Manager in an appliances company

You may think that working in a bank, I might be financia ly more proactive and prudent compared to the average person in another profession. Let me tell you, I was as ignorant about my post-retirement financial planning as any other person. As a single mother, I was constantly shufflin between taking care of my two wonderful kids and my job. Somewhere, I ended up ignoring my retirement planning.

Just 10 years were left. My kids were out of college. One had a job, and one was pursuing further education. I was having a casual conversation with one of my old friends about how we would spend our lives after retirement as I didn't want to stay with my children and be a burden on them. Suddenly we talked about how much money we were going to need, and I was completely crestfallen. It suddenly downed upon me that aside from my provident fund, a single insurance policy and a couple of fi ed deposit accounts, I had no other provisions, especially if I needed to take care of a sudden expense such as sickness or calamity. The same friend suggested me Jigish's name.

Having worked in a bank I totally understand the value of good financial advice. I didn't waste much time and called him up. He gave me a patient hearing and then we set up a meeting.

In 10 years he has been able to completely turn around my savings and investments and I'm looking towards a rich retirement life after two years. With strategic short-term and long-term allocations, he has ensured that my wealth grows fast and even when I'm retired, I will be making as much money as I am making right now, and even more if he goes on working the way he is working with my finances right now. I highly recommend him.

Sarika Agarwal,
Bank Manager

LET'S KEEP TALKING...

My objective is that this book is not the end of conversation, but the initiation of a long-term relationship.

I invite you to continue the discussion by joining me through social media channels mentioned below. Let's share our knowledge with each other and explore this unknown territory together. I also urge you to reach out to me for 30 mins Free Strategy Call on the contact no. given below or set up an appointment with me over a Zoom Call.

Email: jigish@jpfinancial.i

Website: https://jpfinancial.c m

Mobile: +91 9892202415

www.linkedin.com/in/retirementstrategist

www.ingramcontent.com/pod-product-compliance
Ingram Content Group UK Ltd.
Pitfield, Milton Keynes, MK11 3LW, UK
UKHW021654190726
13853UKWH00001B/257

9 789390 828586